"But My Cows Aren't Going To England."

by Sushma Lal and Amrit Wilson

A Study in How Families Are Divided

Hundreds of Asian families are forced to live apart as their applications for entry into Britain are refused by the Entry Clearance Officers (ECOs), on the ground of low credibility.
There is ample evidence to prove that if fair trials were possible, it would be the ECOs whose credibility would fall to pieces. For it is they who practice the ugliest form of deceit, who flout the law, and who rule with the clear motive of practising racism.

Manchester Law Centre

Photographs: Greg Dropkin

Written and researched by Sushma Lal and Amrit Wilson

Published by Manchester Law Centre

© Copyright Manchester Law Centre, 1986

ISBN 0 948969 00 8

Further copies are obtainable at £2.00 (inc. p & p) from:

Manchester Law Centre
584/6 Stockport Road
Longsight
MANCHESTER
M13 0RQ

Bookshop distribution:

Scottish and Northern Book Distribution
18 Granby Row
MANCHESTER
M1 3GE
Telephone: 061-228 3903

Photoset by Onset 061-338 8129
Produced by Iris Services 061-366 6685
Printed by Manchester Free Press 061-236 8822

CONTENTS

Introduction
A Study in How Families Are Divided 6

Part One
**Immigration procedures:
how they work in practice – *Sushma Lal***

Entry Certificate 8
Written Application 9
Place of Interview 9
Interview 11
Family Tree 12
Documentation 14
Income Tax Record 16
Age Assessment 17
Sponsors' interview in the U.K. 18
Agents 18
Refusals 19
Fundamental changes 21

Part Two
Immigration in context – *Amrit Wilson*

Colonialism 23
Plunder 23
Destruction of countryside and towns 25
Different attitudes to the black family and the white family .. 28
Effects of partition 30
Separations 31
Cotton industry in Britain 33
Immigration and neo-colonialism 37
Ibrahim Ali's case 37
How the Home Office polices Bangladesh 39
Racist humiliation through 'medical' tests 49
Paranoia 52

INTRODUCTION

"I came to Britain on my own in 1963, the first few years I spent in Bradford working in a wool mill. I got £9 a week, of which I sent home £6 and somehow managed to live on £3. Then in 1969 I moved to Oldham and got a job in a textile mill. It was very noisy and dusty. It was nightshift work. Before Bangladeshis came to Bradford there was no nightshift work in these factories. All mill workers suffer because of the dust, we have chest ailments which come and go for years and that is what has happened to me too."

Sikandar Ali is taking us to his home to meet his wife. "I had applied to bring my wife and children here in 1978, in December 1982 my wife and one daughter were finally allowed in but the eldest daughter Shahida was left behind. The immigration officers won't believe that she is our daughter. I have so much evidence but they won't believe me. They ask all sorts of irrelevant questions, make crazy accusations. They say how come you are 48 and your brother is 23, it is not possible. You are a liar and you are lying about Shahida. We appealed against the decision and in court they told us that we were too poor. They said "Where will you keep your daughter, what will she eat – that is how kind this government is! As though we parents will push our babies out of doors and let them starve – that is not our culture."

We come to a row of terraced houses on the cold flank of outer Manchester, on the edge of Oldham. Sikandar Ali's house is damp and decrepit. There is a table with papers and a large half open cupboard. His wife comes out. Her eyes fill with tears when I ask about Shahida. She takes a photograph and shows it to me. It is a picture of the whole family. Shahida is a beautiful seventeen year old girl, innocent and vulnerable looking. Her younger sister is here but she got left behind. The mother and daughters are very close – they are the centre of family emotions. Sikandar Ali is in pain, almost bewildered by the tragedy which has befallen them. He says "Here the mother cries, there the daughter cries. I don't know what to do." The mother says "Shahida has been ill, she is alone! She has told the Immigration Adjudicator this but was then told that if she was ill, medical reasons were enough to stop her coming anyway."

Sikandar Ali and his wife come to the door, pressing us to come again. Then we go up the hill to the council estate where Hamdu Miah lives. It is cold and damp to the bone. The evening is drawing in. We are overwhelmed with the question – Why? Why? Why?

*What kind of 'morality' allows Adjudicators and Entry Clearance Officers to place people on trial judging their character and arbitrarily branding them as liars simply because they want to bring their children into a country where they have given so many years of their labour.

*Why is it that despite their contempt for local authorities in Bangladesh and despite their blatant racism the Entry Clearance Officers receive the co-operation of Bangladeshi officials and doctors in humiliating rural Bengali women and destroying the Bengali family.

*The British state has enacted an Immigration law which takes away all people's human rights. In the face of this the same authorities now claim to occasionally exercise their 'compassion'. What does such 'compassion' mean?

*Why do immigration advisers in legal centres, rights centres and so on, advise people to use the appeals system when it is well known that this, the Immigration appeals system, consists of Home Office representatives judging the decisions of other Home Office representatives.

In this pamphlet we look at some of these isues as illustrated by the experiences of Bangladeshi families divided by British immigration laws. We show how the exclusion of families is the latest step in the plain exploitation of a people exploited for generations. And we examine how this particular struggle of workers in Britain against immigration laws links up with colonialism and neo-colonialism.

Each of us is responsible for the views expressed in the sections we have ourselves written.

Amrit Wilson and Sushma Lal
October 1985

Part One
Immigration procedures: how they work in practice.

The right to family life is one of the most fundamental rights recognised by the civilised world. It is respected by English law and, of course, is recognised by numerous international agreements and conventions to which Britain is a signatory. It is generally believed that the black immigrants settled in this country are not excluded. The Immigration Act 1971 gives a right to all male British citizens irrespective of their country of origin and colour of skin to bring their wives and unmarried children under 18 to join them here.

That is the theory. In practice the Home Office has devised a system by which it makes sure that as few black families enter the country as possible.

The aim is achieved by:
(i) bringing a rule under the delegated powers of the Home Minister which requires the families to obtain entry certificates in their country of residence before the start of the journey and then
(ii) simply by refusing to accept the claimed relationship.

Entry Certificate
The entry certificate requirement was made mandatory in 1969 by the Wilson government with the objective of avoiding unnecessary distress to families, who used to get stranded at London Airport whilst undergoing investigation.

Protests in London

The truth was that at the airport the families had better access to legal facilities and their cases were attended to more swiftly. Under the present system, families have to wait several years (sometimes a decade) before their cases are scrutinised and decided upon. It is clear that the entry clearance system has failed to achieve either a more humane system or improved efficiency. Indeed it is not disputed that delays in the finalisation of cases are greater than ever before, inflicting suffering on innocent women and children whilst there is no evidence that more bogus applicants are being detected.

Application

In order to obtain entry certificate, a Bangladeshi family must make a written application, on a prescribed form, to the British High Commission in Dhaka. Originally the forms were free of charge but the Thatcher government has, for the first time, now introduced a fee of Taka 420 (£10) per entry certificate. The fee is exorbitantly high, especially considering the financial position of the applicants, who may well belong to the lowest earning group in Bangladesh.

Place of Interview

The interviews are held in Dhaka, whereas most of the applicants live in the Sylhet district, at a distance similar to that of London and Newcastle. The similarity, however, ends there. The difficulties which the Bangladeshi families encounter in making this journey will probably be inconceivable for people in the West. The roads are almost non-existent and public transport by no means satisfactory. The situation is better explained by an ECO, in his village visit report:

> "There are no roads in the area and nothing in the way of accommodation and it would only be possible for officers of this mission to attempt to visit to that region in the cooler dry season between December and February.
>
> During the week beginning 17th January 1977 my colleagues Mr. J.C. Gough and Mr. D.A. Dell, accompanied by two Sylheti born interpreters, a driver and a cook, made a visit to the Sylhet District and made strenuous but unsuccessful efforts to reach the village of Mr. A. The village was inaccessible because the dirt road leading to the main river crossing had been washed away and was still not repaired. On reaching the Jagannathpur District, the team spent seven hours trying alternative routes by Landrover and on foot, but eventually had to give up at a point ten miles from the village. It was therefore decided that a further effort would be made to reach the area during the week beginning 14th February 1977."

A client of mine, Mr. A. described his ordeal to the High Commission as follows:

He comes from a village called Halidpur in the Jagannathpur area. He, with his wife and three children, set off at about 6 o'clock in the morning. His home being about 3 miles from any kind of transport, they had to walk that distance to the river. At the river he had to get the big boat which took 1½ hours to cross to the bus station. The bus took another three hours to reach Sylhet town. There, they got a train at 8 o'clock in the evening, which got to Dhaka at 9 o'clock in the morning the next day. There was no question of getting any sleep all through the journey. They were exhausted.

The High Commission was about five miles away. It was already too late for the interview as they had been asked to be present at the gate by 7.30 in the morning.

He had to look for a hotel and hire two rooms as only three persons were allowed in one room. Next day he had to catch a taxi, as it was not possible for him to seek accommodation in the very expensive area where the High Commission was. By the time he finished the interview (he was lucky) it was 2.00 p.m. There was no train back to Sylhet until the next morning. So he had to stay another night in the hotel. He then got a train back to Sylhet at 8.00 a.m. (only one train a day) repeating the whole exhausting journey and reached home the next day.

The families do not have to make this journey only once. Another client of mine, Mr. Chowdhry, like many others, had to go through the process three times. In his case, he applied for entry for his family, consisting of a wife and three children on 11th May 1977. They were called for their first interview on 2nd August 1979, which they attended with their new baby born on 5th March 1979. The interview was suspended for want of an income tax record. A second interview was held on 18th August 1980 but deferred again for a village visit. The family was interviewed again on 20th May 1981 when entry certificates were granted to all except the two older boys.

The callousness and disregard of the applicants' needs becomes even more apparent if one compares the conditions of the ECO's with those of the Bangladeshi families. The journey was found impossible by the ECO (See earlier) despite being young, well fed, used to travelling and having every modern facility to hand. The applicants who are necessarily women (often pregnant) and young children who have probably never been out of their village before, are expected to struggle through by means of public transport.

The possibility of opening an office in Sylhet has been taken up with the Home Office by various Labour M.P.s and other organisations connected with immigration. The proposal has fallen on deaf ears. The C.R.E. was given the following reasons for refusal:

a) Difficulty in communicating between Dhaka and Sylhet, particularly by telephone.
b) That there was no suitable building to house the registry.

c) That the staff would lose morale and suffer from isolation and lack of facilities.
d) Difficulty in consulting related files.

One ECO summed up the objections to the C.R.E. by arguing that there would be no advantage in a move "other than making the logistics of applicants coming to us easier".

Recently the question was raised in the House of Commons by Mr. Peter Bruinvels, Labour M.P. Mr. Renton, the Minister responsible replied:

> "I have considered the matter carefully, particularly since my visit to Bangladesh in January. Applicants come from the large Sylhet district, not only from Sylhet town, and Dhaka is more convenient than Sylhet town for many of them. The journey from Sylhet to Dhaka is not expensive and there are good road, rail and air links. The problem for most applicants is getting from their village to Sylhet and not from Sylhet to Dhaka. Operational problems relating to the opening of the office would be formidable and I cannot accept that the expenditure on such a project would be justified."

The Minister's verdict is a complete mystery to the Bangladeshis.

It is true that the majority of the applicants do not live in Sylhet town proper, but almost 95% live in the Sylhet district. To catch a train for Dhaka, they have to go to Sylhet first. If an office was opened in Sylhet, the applicants, many of whom are already exhausted from travelling, would be saved a 20-hour train journey.

Interview

When the families arrive at the High Commission, they are taken to a waiting room. It is furnished with wooden benches with a small desk near the door for the receptionist. The difference between that room and the rest of the building, where the proper High Commission staff sit, is similar to that between the lounge and the cellar of an ordinary house. The whole of the building is air conditioned except the waiting room. There are only two toilets (one male and one female) with no facilities for changing babies. It must be remembered that some families will have to wait in that waiting room for a whole day before their turn for interview comes.

In these conditions the procedure normally goes like this: By 8 o'clock the only thing that has happened is that passports have been collected for scrutiny. At about 8.30 a white man will come down with a local person and shout out some names. Eventually a family will be taken upstairs. They will then be called in (individually) for interview. Every care is taken that each person, including the children is kept away from the others in case some valuable information is

Members of divided families, angry with the High Commission

passed over. The procedure is very much like a criminal trial where witnesses are interrogated and kept apart until they have given evidence. The difference, of course, is that at the trial the accused has a legal representative in court to look after his interests. In the High Commission the ECOs are both prosecutors and judges, whilst the families have no one whatsoever to take care of their interests.

Family Tree

The interview begins with the obtaining of the family tree. This is an ingenious catch. Each and every applicant, sometimes even friends and distant relatives who happen to be accompanying the family, are asked to give names, relationship and ages of real and step grand parents, parents, uncles, aunts, their children and the children of their children with their sexes and ages. This includes living and deceased relatives. The questions are specific but nevertheless people miss out some names or give different ones and most certainly get mixed up with the ages. There are various reasons for this. There is room for confusion and misinterpretation. The exercise is boring and tedious and most of all the applicants fail to see the connection between their application to go to the U.K. and the names of the dead relatives.

Whatever the reasons for any discrepancies the question must arise whether this line of questioning really does help in establishing the relationships. Let us hear direct from the horse's mouth. A directive from the Home Office states:

> "A family tree is taken in all first interviews. This is not, however, a test which can be relied upon to expose well-prepared bogus applicants since they might know the family very well anyway and would be well drilled. For the same reason, do not rely upon it, as genuine applicants can make mistakes in giving the family tree which could later be very difficult to account for".

Therefore, if the Home Office acknowledged itself that the bogus applicants, who in many cases are alleged to be close relatives, will know the family tree, then what is the point of spending all this time on questioning about the family tree? and why are hundreds of applications refused on this basis?

There is unanimous agreement amongst all the persons and organisations who have anything to do with immigration that the family tree method proves nothing and is a sheer waste of time. Yet to ask the Home Office to give up questioning regarding the family tree is like taking away the bone from a dog. As a matter of fact the Home Office's devotion to the family tree is understandable. Family tree discrepancies are easy to find and can easily be built up to make the case look ridiculous to use as a reason for refusing entry. The object is to look for excuses for refusal not proof of relationships. The family tree method has been such a success in denying entry to Asian families that it has now been introduced in fiances' and visitors' interviews as well.

The Bangladeshis, realising that they were being conned by the ECOs into this trap, tried to counteract by shortening their family trees (called pruning). They thought that the less they had to say the fewer would be the discrepancies. This tactic did not prove to be effective. The ultimate power being with the ECOs, they simply refused to accept a family tree which fell short of their expectations or, in other words, which did not give them enough to get their teeth into.

If the ECO has not amused himself enough by now then he will go on to ask (a) how many windows are there in the sponsor's house, (b) what sort of sleeping arrangements they have (c) how many cows and chickens they possess.

In one instance a woman found strength to inform the ECO that her cows were not going to England, nevertheless, it did not deter him from asking her further similar nonsensical questions. Obviously, it is not necessary to be a wife or son to know the answers to such questions. Equally, any error in replies does not prove the non existence of the claimed relationship. The exercise is a farce. Yet it goes on with the greatest vigour on the part of the Home Office.

A further set of questions may be to enquire (a) who attended a particular family wedding, (b) who went to see the sponsor off or to receive him from the airport (this could be as long as five years ago) (c) how many visits to Bangladesh the sponsor has made since his emigration to Britain, etc. Frequently the replies do not tally, and the application is refused.

A friend of mine, who is a vicar in Oldham, after reading one of the explanatory statements, told me that he had tried a comparable experiment with his family. At Christmas, he was at his parents-in-law's home. Some other close relatives were also present. The next day he asked everybody to name the people who had been present the night before. The result was even worse than he had expected. Most people had failed to name one or more guests.

Finally, the ECO may choose to ask the applicant to explain why there is a gap between the births of the children. To quote from one of the ECO's files, the following instruction is given to the Immigration Officer in London:

> "Ask the sponsor if he can explain the gap in his child fathering between (first child) and (second child). It was during this period that he first went to the U.K. but he made a visit back to Bangladesh from 28th October 1966 to 22 July 1967, yet no children were born as a result of that visit."

So the Bangladeshis not only have to satisfy the ECOs about the actual applicants, but also have to satisfy them about children never born to them.

Documentation

Basically, ECOs' attitude towards the documentation in Bangladesh is that they are not worth the paper they are written on. The UKIAS and CRE reports confirm this. The following extract from one of the Home Office statements will illustrate the point:

> "I then came to consider the application. I found that I was not satisfied that the applicants were related to sponsor because ....
> (a) A copy of a land deed with English translation. I had not been shown the original of this document. This copy had been drawn up on 25.11.79 possibly with this application in mind. Unfortunately, such documents are easily available to wealthy sponsors and their value is diminished as a result.
> (b) School certificate in respect of Ashraf Mia and certificate from the Chairman of the Union Council. Unfortunately, it is again the case that wealthy sponsors (who earn more in a week than does a Bangladeshi local government officer in a year) can easily obtain such documents and I did not feel able to attach any great weight to them."

Nevertheless, it is common that cases are deferred for want of documentation. Here is one example:

> "Mr. Palmer then questioned the sponsor on matters relating to his first marriage and the subsequent divorce. He stated that he married Jahanara Begum in 1955 but he had no marriage deed. He stated that he had submitted an affidavit to the Inland Revenue in support of his claim for the tax relief. Mr. Palmer then asked the sponsor if he was able to produce any other documentary evidence relating to his first marriage e.g. old family correspondence or remittance receipts. He stated that he had no other documents to produce in support of the application. Mr. Palmer, therefore, deferred the application in order that inquiries be made of the Inland Revenue in order to ascertain what documentary evidence, if any, had been produced to that department regarding the first marriage and subsequent divorce."

One can see that the sponsor is saying clearly that he does not have and never had any documentary proof of his marriage, yet the ECO decides to defer the interview.

Later in the same case, he goes on to reject the application and lists the reasons for refusal as follows:

> "No marriage deed had been produced and no explanation had been offered as to why such a document was not available."

and in the same breath, further on in the text, he says:

> "With regard to the Divorce Deed, Mr. Palmer was aware of the case with which such documents can be fraudulently obtained in Bangladesh. He was therefore reluctant to place any evidential value on this document."

Can anyone beat this line of argument?

In addition, the guidance leaflet issued with the application form clearly sets out the document which the applicants should bring with them or explicitly stating that failure to produce the documents requested may lead to delays and difficulties. Finally, it warns against producing false documents.

It is, therefore, clear that there is a considerable pressure on applicants to produce documents. Yet the evidential value awarded to these documents is nil. Why the pressure? The reason is simple. Firstly, if the document asked for does not exist, the applicants feel pressure to get one forged. This will bring an element of forgery into the case and give good grounds for refusal.

Secondly, even if the documents are genuine, they will provide additional material to check against the oral statements. This will create further opportunities for discrepancies to be discovered, thus providing extra grounds for refusal.

The following is a very interesting example of the approach the ECOs take towards documentation. The case is of a Mr. R., who came to England in 1962. He applied again in 1982 and produced a land deed in favour of his wife wherein he was referred to as her husband. The ECO had this to say:

> "The land deed at Appendix B bore a date stamp indicating it had been produced at this office on 24th June 1969 but the principal applicant denied having applied for entry certificate before and had no explanation to offer as to how the land deed had come to be stamped in this way.... As the ECO was interested to know why the land deed bore the British High Commission stamp he decided to ask Home Office to interview the sponsor in the U.K. The sponsor was interviewed in London and he could offer no explanation."

It was clear that the sponsor, being illiterate, could not connect the stamp with his application in 1969 and therefore could not offer any explanation. The application was refused on the ground that the sponsor and his wife were liars.

The irony is that no attempt whatsoever was made by the ECO or the adjudicator to ascertain the genuineness of the deed itself. Emphasis, all through, had been on the British High Commission stamp. It was never explained how their own stamp rendered the deed invalid.

Income Tax Record

The tax record, when obtained is compared with the family tree produced earlier on. If any discrepancies are found, the applicants are grilled and their application refused. There are two points which need explaining:

1. Until 1968, the time when most of the primary immigration from Bangladesh took place, it was incredibly easy to claim income tax relief for dependants overseas. All one had to do was to produce an affidavit in support of the existence of the dependants, and a few remittance receipts to prove financial support. In the majority of cases the income tax returns were completed by some wise men of the community and frequently, false claims were put in. In many cases this was futile as the claimants were on such a low income that their own dependants were sufficient to exhaust the relief their income could take.

Now the High Commission, having found out about that, use it to maximum effect not only to refuse the application but also to humiliate women and children by declaring them to be of low credibility and, of course, not worthy to live in a civilised country like England.

The trick works on the basis that the sponsors are asked to give information about children who are not seeking admission. As the sponsors know that their income tax will be checked, they have two options. Firstly, they may stick to the information provided to the Revenue 10/12 years ago, in which case they have to account for the missing children (that is, those not now applying).

The ECO's questioning about the non-applicant children pushes the applicants deeper and deeper into his trap. In attempting to dispose of non-applicant children, they end up with an interview obtained with false statements and discrepancies. The ECO's job becomes so much easier: he declares everybody of low credibility, refuses the application and goes happily home.

The other alternative is to confess. In many cases no doubt they do. But then the ECO's argument for rejecting the application changes to the following: If the sponsor has been lying for so many years, his credibility must be doubted. There is no reason to believe that he has told the truth now. So, heads we win, tails you lose!

In every civilised society, young and innocent are protected. Yet, in immigration, the Home Office punishes women and children who have played no part whatsoever in the avoiding of tax responsibilities by the sponsor.

Age Assessment

Frequently ECOs declare that they do not agree with applicants' claimed ages and refer them to British High Commission medical officer for their ages to be assessed medically. The reason is not, as one might imagine, that they suspect the applicant child to be over the age limit or too old to be the sponsor's child. The object of this act is simply to prove that the applicants are liars and that they are covering up the family declared in income tax record. For example, the woman applicant's age is assessed to establish, not that she is not the sponsor's wife but that she is standing in place of the wife claimed in the income tax record. The CRE reports the following extacts from the High Commission files:

> "I am not going to accept this arrant nonsense anymore – she is clearly a lot younger than 37 and cannot be the mother of the non-applicant children."

The wife was sent for medical examination and her age was assessed to be 30 whereas she claimed to be 37.

It is clear the ECO is not doubtful about the relationship (which he should be concentrating upon) but about the non-applicant family, which should not be his concern anyway.

The age assessment business is not only useless but manifestly obscene and degrading. Internal examination is an essential part of the age assessment whereas there is no provision of women medical officers. One case report makes it clear that after having her *skull examined, teeth counted and pubic hair vetted,* (by a male doctor) the woman was declared to be 37 whereas she claimed to be 40 and she was disqualified for entry.

In the period of slavery similar methods were used to evaluate the price of slaves. Currently such practices are justified by the Home Office to keep British culture intact. There is, however, a difference. The slaves did not have to pay. The Bangladeshis have to pay 100 Takas per report.

Sponsors interview in U.K.

Sponsors are interviewed in England at various ports. The interviews are suspended during the summer months, as the Immigration Officers are busy, and therefore considerable time is added to the finalisation of the application. This generally consists of obtaining confirmation of the details which were obtained in Bangladesh. i.e. going through the family tree (a must!) and similar nonsensical questions. Sometimes it turns into an inquiry into the sponsor's own status in the U.K.

Mr. L. applied for his family's entry on 22nd July 1977. On 28th June 1978, his house in Oldham was raided at 7 o'clock in the morning by 2 men and one woman immigration officers. They searched his home including other tenants' belongings, arrested him, took him to Birmingham. He was kept in custody for 2 days and one night. They found nothing and cleared him. In 1982 he went to Bangladesh in order to attend the interview at the High Commission with his family. The ECO took his passport and refused to return it. After repeated visits made by Mr. L. to the High Commission for the return of his passport, he was able to get it back but it was cancelled. He was told no further passport would be issued as he was an illegal immigrant. It was not until Manchester Law Centre took the matter up with the Home Office that the charge was withdrawn on 13th December 1984 and he was issued with a passport in January 1985.

Mr. L. arrived back in U.K. in February 1985 and is awaiting a decision on his family's appeal.

Agents

The High Commission, in order to show the interest of people to emigrate to England argue that there are many agents working in Bangladesh who charge a large amount of money to facilitate gaining entry. The truth is that the High Commission has managed to make the system so difficult and ordinary people feel so scared, that they feel compelled to go to agents. Their reason for this is not that the application is bogus but that dealing with the High Commission is complicated and confusing. They do not wish to endanger their family's entry. Therefore even for genuine children a lot of sponsors are compelled to use agents.

In support of their claim the British High Commission also boasts about a "confession register" they maintain. This contains statements which have been extracted from sponsors about so-called "bogus children". It is claimed that in 1982, 340 confessions involving 1,000 children were made. Only on close scrutiny will it transpire that the register is so maintained that it tends to mislead and represents an inflated figure of bogus children who would have gained entry illegally had the High Commission not been so diligent. The truth of the matter is that 85% of the children subjected to confession had merely been listed on the application as other children, and were never applicants for entry to Britain.

Refusals

The figures provided to the Select Committee on Race Relations and Immigration by the Home Office show that in 1983 applications for settlement from wives and children from Bangladesh were decided as follows:

Wives

Granted	Refused
3,840	1,690

Children

Granted	Refused
4,260	5,380

On the other hand, various investigations have been carried out by independent organisations and their findings are as follows:

Runnymede Trust: Out of 58 cases refused by the ECO and also rejected on appeal all but 3 were in fact genuine.

UKIAS: (a Home Office funded body) Out of 45 cases only 3 were not satisfactorily resolved.

Manchester Law Centre: 18 cases were investigated involving 11 wives and 51 children. All the wives were genuine; only 4 children were not born of the same parents as claimed.

In addition numerous individuals have carried out investigations and they have all concluded that most of the applications refused are genuine. Moreover almost all other organisations which have had any connection with the immigrant community agree unanimously that a large number of genuine wives and children are being refused entry, causing great distress and hardship to innocent people.

The discrepancy between the findings of the ECOs and other organisations which are by no means all left wing lunatics (e.g. UKIAS) is such that it would be hard to maintain that there is not something fundamentally wrong with the system used by the Home Office for granting entry certificates. The Home Office insists that the present system is the best that they could have. They are correct. If the purpose of the system is to regulate the number of people coming into the country with utter disregard for the distress it causes to innocent women and children, then the system is an ingenious one. If the purpose is to apply the law both in letter and in spirit, then it is the most ridiculous and appalling system ever conceived.

The explanation given by the Home Office in support of the current system is that attempts to evade control have been extensive and systematic and therefore it is necessary to take great care in ensuring that bogus applicants do not secure entry. They argue that the evasion is a direct result of the pressure of poverty existing in the sub-continent. An average Bangladeshi is prepared to pay a large sum of money to achieve entry into Britain. Furthermore they maintain that the social system in the sub-continent is such that the family is close-knit and that a prosperous member is expected to look after the less fortunate ones in it. Therefore, the Bangladeshis in England will feel a responsibility to bring their brother's or sister's child into this country by fair means or foul.

The above reasoning is ridiculously simple, sweeping and superficial. As far as the wives are concerned, none of the above arguments will hold water. The women in question are illiterate and in their late 40s, and the clear evidence is that such women do not go out to work in England. Financially, it costs more to keep them in the UK than in Bangladesh and socially it is extremely embarrassing for a woman to present herself as the wife of a man who is not in fact her husband. Finally, the most important factor which is never mentioned by the Home Office is that these sponsors, who are in their 40s are more likely to be married than not and, if so, why on earth would they choose to bring in someone else's wife and leave their own back in Bangladesh? The irony is that in Home Office statements it is frequently claimed that it is usual for Bangladeshis to have larger families yet they refuse to accept that the Bangladeshis already in this country can have even one wife and a few children of their own.

As far as the children are concerned, no-one denies that attempts have been made when a sponsor in this country has tried to bring in his brother's or sister's child. This, however, does not occur on a scale that could justify the outrageously high refusal rate operated by the Home Office. The cost to the applicant both in time and money is high. In many cases the sponsors have incurred high fees for legal representation, which would offset any financial gain they were going to have in bringing in so-called bogus children. Furthermore, they have to go through the gruelling interviews, then give evidence at appeal, which is equally unpleasant. Most of all the sponsors know very well that if the ECO suspects anything in the case, his whole family is going to be refused entry. Therefore, there will be very few people prepared to go to the length of including with their own application a bogus applicant to the prejudice of their own family's entry...

It is clear that the problems these families are facing are not primarily legal but are relative to the administration of the current law by the Home Office. Therefore, proposals being made in various quarters regarding changes in rules of evidence or burden of proof, though worthy of support, are not going to change the situation drastically. These sorts of changes have not helped in the past and there is no reason to suppose that they are going to make any difference in the future. For example, after much protest and agitation, the Home Office agreed to stop using the STP (Sylhet Tax Pattern – a document used by the Home Office and attached to all divided family explanatory statements, alleging tax fraud was rife in Sylhet) but, as the CRE report confirms, it has not made any difference whatsoever in the working of the ECOs. Similarly, in 1982, the Home Office agreed to disregard a discrepancy of up to 6/7 years in the age assessment but in practice it is still held adversely against the applicants.

If there is any doubt remaining about the horrific treatment of applicants then the following extracts from British High Commission files must prove conclusive to establish what is in fact going on in Dacca.

A note by an ECO, warning other ECOs not to handle a particular case he was dealing with, says:

"I want to do this reinterview myself. Hands Off". The senior officers are not displeased: *"Well done, looks as if you've hit the jackpot again."*

Another ECO says:

"This must be this year's strongest refusal."

The following note will bring out the pain felt by an ECO just at the thought of issuing an entry certificate.

"Sponsor agreed to age estimate on principal applicant and child, then said he did not have enough money. I was tempted to refuse but it would be painfully thin. Therefore, defer application for sponsor to produce his passport and for possible tax check. I may have to issue here, but draw the line at including a bogus boy. Sponsor may decide in the interview to tell the truth."

Fundamental Changes

It is clear that something more fundamental is needed than just procedural changes. In order to achieve any meaningful result, there are two proposals which can be put forward:

A simple, short and sensible solution would be to grant entry certificate to all the wives and children who are on the waiting list now.

> a) Most of these applicants have been in the merry-go-round for a decade or so. The period of time they have spent in going backward and forward to the High Commission in itself is evidence of the fact that they are genuinely related to the men in the U.K.
>
> b) All developed countries have had immigration from the Indian sub-continent. None of them deny family rights to persons who have already been accepted for settlement. No other country has found reasons to maintain such queues or refuse applications on the ground of relationship. If others can fulfil their legal obligations then there is no justification that Britain could not.

Another solution to the problem can be achieved by bringing in changes in the present appeal system. Ordinarily a good appeal system should serve two purposes: (a) to deter the executive from exceeding their powers and (b) to provide impartial and objective reviews of the cases.

The present immigration appeal system neither deters the executive nor provides reviews. It is clear from the appallingly low success rate of appeals, and from the cases referred to earlier in the text which had been to appeal and had been refused. Persons connected with these appeals will confirm that the appellate authorities tend to adopt the same line of reasoning as the ECOs and frequently take political considerations into account when delivering decisions.

Indeed, it has been a long-standing criticism of the immigration appeals that members of the appellate body are hired and can be fired only by the Home Office who is a party to each and every case which they decide. Fundamental principles of justice are blatantly eroded in the appeal system provided to the immigrants.

It is therefore suggested that the power of appointment should rest with the Lord Chancellor's Department, as is the case of other judicial appointments.

As there is a human element in all immigration cases it is further suggested that one member of the Immigration Tribunal should be appointed from a panel maintained by an independent organisation (such as the British Council of Churches).

Part Two
Immigration in context

COLONIALISM

In the seventeenth century Bengal was one of the most beautiful and advanced regions in the world. Not only was it remarkably fertile but it had a well-balanced and vigorous economy and a culture rich with the creativity and art of its people.

It had cities which were great commercial centres but (as travellers noted) "in even the smallest villages rice, flour, butter, milk, beans and other vegetables, sugar and other sweetmeats, dry and liquid, were to be found in abundance". It exported cotton, silk, rice, sugar and butter and "produced amply for its own consumption, wheat, vegetables, grains, fowl, ducks and geese. It has immense herds of pigs and flocks of sheep and goats. Fish of every kind it has in profusion. From Rajmahal to the sea is an endless number of canals, cut in bygone ages from the Ganges by immense labour, for navigation and irrigation."[1]

Britain's relationship with this region began with trade, with the merchants of the East India Company trying to make a profit by securing a monopoly in the goods and products of India. But in this they faced a major problem – England in the seventeenth century had nothing of value which Indians might want to buy or exchange. In fact the only important industry in England at that time was the manufacture of woollen goods – products which were of no use in India.

Plunder

As a result the merchants were forced to buy Indian goods with precious metals. At the time (the days of mercantile capitalism) the real worth of a country was measured in the amount of precious metal it owned, so this system was not thought to be to the benefit of England. The East India Company then turned its attention to finding means of forcibly altering this arrangement to the terms of trade they desired. In other words they turned to plunder – taking commodities and giving nothing in return.

India at this time was going through a period of political instability and vulnerability – the Mogul empire was breaking up and with it the administrative structure of that empire. The British took advantage of this situation and using their one asset – superior military strength and technology – gained military domination over Bengal. The terms of trade were then transformed. What took place now in the words of an English merchant was as follows:[2]

1. Tavernier, Travels in India, OUP 1925.
2. Palme Dutt, India Today, Manisha Granthalaya.

"The English with their Banyans and black Gomastahs arbitrarily decide what quantities of goods each manufacturer shall deliver and the prices he shall receive for them... the assent of the poor weaver is in general not deemed necessary; for the Gomastahs when employed on the company's investment, frequently make them sign what they please; and upon the weavers refusing to take the money offered, it has been known that they have been tied up in their girdles and they have been sent away with a flogging... A number of these weavers are generally also registered in the books of the company's Gomastahs and not permitted to work for any others, being transferred from one to another as so many slaves... the roguery practised in this department is beyond imagination; but all terminates in the defrauding of the poor weaver for the prices... at least 15% and some even 40% less that the goods so manufactured would sell in the public bazaar or the market upon free sale". In Sylhet itself, as records of the period show, the situation was no different from the rest of Bengal. It was a part of the country comparatively well-protected by forests and mountains. One contemporary report[3] describes the land near the main town. "Near the town of Sylhet the country presents a novel appearance being composed of various conical shaped hills with broad bases rising irregularly at short distances from each other and covered with trees and verdure to the very summit while to the North and East lofty mountains rise abruptly like a wall and appear as if at some remote period they had withstood the surge of the ocean."

"During the rains a great proportion of the land is laid under water by the overflowing of the Soormah and other rivers by which it is intersected, so that the passage from Dacca is performed for nearly the whole way over rice and pasture fields which in the cold season are many feet above the current of the rivers. Over this tract, when the floods are at their height, there is eight or twelve feet of water; the elevated sites of the villages appear like islands; the very masts are entangled among the branches of trees, while their progress is impeded by the matted thickness and adhesion of paddy stalks. When the innundation drains off the land is left in an excellent condition for rice cultivation, which species of food is so abundant that rice in the husk sold for fifteen rupees per one hundred maunds of eighty pounds each and coarser grains were cheaper still. In addition to this ample supply, every stream and puddle swarms with fish." In the 17th century Sylhet was a producer not only of rice but sugar cotton, oranges, limes, wax, aguru or fragrant aloe wood, silk and iron goods.

Despite its natural defences the British merchants managed to arrive in Sylhet by the latter half of the 18th century, soon they were using military force. District Records show that the local Rajahs resisted the Company's onslaught. For example a letter to John Shakespeare, Provincial Council of Dacca, describes the need for a Fort to 'protect' the 'trade' at Ponduah.[4] "The

3. Bengal Gazateer, India Office.
4. Bengal Gazateer, India Office.

merchants residing at Ponduah under the protection of the Hon. Company have presented to me that they have lately, not only been insulted, but sustained considerable losses by the Hill Rajahs, compelled by them to dispose of their goods at an arbitrary price, and have requested of me to take some steps towards protecting them from the like grievances in the future. It is unnecessary for me to inform you that the trade carried on between Calcutta and Ponduah has always been considered an object worth the attention of the administration etc.... But for some time past a large number of low Europeans residing at Ponduah, by admitting the petty Rajahs to be their superiors rather than equals, have taught them to consider themselves totally independent of the Company and infused into them a spirit of independence which if not checked will be a means of putting a stop to the trade of that market."

The means of checking it was military power, through this they took over (by 1765) the administration of Bengal, Bihar and Orissa. After this 'revenue' was added to the plunder from trade. In addition the British took over the best land for cash crops, forcing the peasants to surrender it through the most violent methods which included rape, arson and torture. Profit was the main consideration. In 1765, reports of the East India Company show that of the total revenue of Bengal, only a quarter was spent on the expenses of government and another quarter was paid to Indian feudal rulers; a half was clear profit to the Company. Between 1765 and 1793 the land revenue of Bengal rose from £1,470,000 to £3,400,000.

Destruction of Countryside and Towns

The effects of these ever increasing revenues was a destruction of the countryside. Peasants had to sell their bullocks and even their seed corn in their efforts to pay taxes, and often even that was not enough. Food production slumped, famines of an intensity never seen before became a periodic phenomena. Meanwhile (as Warren Hastings recorded in 1772)[5] "Not withstanding the loss of at least one third of the inhabitants of the province and the consequent decrease in cultivation the net collection of the year 1771 exceeded even those of 1756.... It was naturally to be expected that the diminution of the revenue should have an equal pace with the other consequences of so great a calamity. That it did not was owing to its being violently kept up to its former standard."

While the first phase of British colonialism destroyed the countryside and depopulated rural areas and weakened the peasantry, the accumulation of capital in England as a result led to the development of modern capitalism in Britain. This in turn required the systematic devastation of towns in Bengal and in fact all over India. It required too the transformation of India from a country whose industries and commodities were some of the most advanced and sought after, to a producer of raw materials for British factories and a consumer of British factory-made goods.

5. Palme Dutt, India Today, Manisha Granthalaya.

Village Life

On the face of it the period from about 1760 to 1790 was one when the creative genius flourished in Britain. There were a series of industrially important inventions from the spinning Jenny in 1764 to the steam engine in 1768 to the power loom in 1785. But any age of inventions requires not just the creativity of the people but enough capital and a market to use these inventions on a large scale. And in Britain this capital was suddenly available from the plunder of India. The battle of Plassey (1757), which effectively gave Britain control over Bengal, was a milestone in that the 50 years which preceded it had seen relatively slow economic growth in Britain, and the fifty years following it saw rapid economic development and expansion.

The cotton industry was a major contributor to this economic growth. On the one hand plunder from India directly fuelled the mills and factories in Britain, on the other the colonialists were in a position to dominate, control and finally destroy Indian cotton production through the imposition of heavy tariffs on Indian imports to Britain (Indian cottons paid 10%, silks 20% and woollen goods 30%, while British cotton and silk goods imported to India paid only 3½%), and secondly by the prevention of trade between India and other European countries. Between 1815 and 1832 Indian cotton goods exported fell to $^1/_{13}$th of their value, while English cotton goods imported went up 16-fold. India, which had exported cotton goods all over the world, became the chief consumer of cotton of British factories. The same process was repeated in the cae of silk, iron, pottery, glass and so on.

The result was the devastation of Indian cities and industrial centres. Towns like Murshidabad and Dacca which Clive had described in 1757 to be "as extensive, populous and rich as the City of London" were, as Palme-Dutt explains, "in a few years rendered desolate under the 'pax Britannica' with a completeness which no ravages of the most destructive war or foreign conquest could have accomplished."

Urban families who had lived for generations in the towns, finding themselves without employment or source of livelihood, fled to rural areas to the land owned by other parts of their extended families. The population of Dacca fell from 150,000 at the beginning of the 19th century to 3-4,000 in 1840. The jungle encroached on streets and markets once full of life and activity. And it was not just the towns, because economically they were not separate entities. They formed the focus of village areas all around, so their collapse meant the beginning of destruction of the entire village economy. Potters, weavers, spinners, metal workers and other crafts people all over Bengal lost their markets. Unemployment haunted the villages. Not only the urban familes who migrated en masse to the countryside, but village crafts families too fell back on agriculture for survival, and the land, although so rich and productive, could not bear the strains upon it. It was the beginning of what is now nearly 200 years later, a cliché – India's rural poverty. India was pushed backwards in a quick succession of steps – first the devastation of the urban economy, secondly the migration of industrial and crafts workers to the villages, thirdly the massive unemployment of rural crafts workers, fourthly the growing poverty in the overburdened countryside; and finally the exacerbation of this oppression by a characteristic form of colonial thuggery – the forcible take over of the best land to grow cash crops. That is why it is incorrect to say that India was 'underdeveloped' by colonialism. It was a society pushed from the verge of developing its own industrial capitalism back into mainly feudal relationships tied up entirely with agricultural production of various kinds.

In the same period Britain was going through a period of unprecedented industrial growth and a total change of lifestyle for its people. For us this period is of particular interest because it saw the establishment of the cotton mills in which so many Bangladeshi workers were to spend thir working lives in the 1970s and 80s. In a later section we shall look at the conditions of the mills in those early days but here we must examine briefly another issue of crucial interest for our purposes. What was the attitude of the British establishment to the white working class family in those early days and how did it differ from the attitude to the black family?

Different Attitudes to the Black Family and the White Family

In Britain the industrial revolution brought a drastic change in the lives of the people. The peasant population were pushed off the land and into the mills and factories. At the beginning women, children and men were all put to work, often in different work places under the most appallingly unpleasant and dangerous conditions. The effects were as Engels describes[6] "A pretty list of diseases engendered purely by the hateful money greed of the manufacturers! Women made unfit for child bearing, children deformed, men enfeebled, limbs crushed, whole generations wrecked, afflicted with diseases and infirmity purely to fill the purses of the bourgeoisie. And when one reads of the barbarism of single cases, how children are seized naked in bed by the overlookers and driven with blows and kicks to the factory, their clothing over their arms... how many hundreds came home so tired that they could eat no supper for sleepiness and want of appetite... how can one be otherwise than filled with wrath and resentment against a class which boasts of philanthropy and self sacrifice while its one object is to fill its purse." Appalling and inhuman though these conditions are, the situation of workers in India was far worse, particularly in the long term. For one thing British workers were in the heart of a capitalist economy enjoying a long phase of vigorous growth, which inevitably was to improve the standard of living of the whole country, they were not like the workers in India, slaves within an economic system whose whole aim was to syphon capital out of their country into Britain.

6. Engels, The Condition of the Working Class in England, Lawrence and Wishart.

For our purposes there was also another crucial difference between workers in Britain in the 19th century and workers in India and this was the fact that the latter were seen as completely expendable. This difference can be understood by looking at the different attitudes to the black and the white family both historically and now. The appalling situation of the workers in 19th Century Britain, their ill health and the fact that the family as an institution was falling apart, led the employers to fear that there would be a shortage of workers in the next generation; the result was that the employers were willing to do something to improve conditions. Given that male workers were better organised, the idea of the Family Wage came into being. This Family Wage, although extremely low, had the effect of pushing women back into the home to 'preserve' the family in order to produce a future generation of workers for capitalism. In India, death and destruction did not matter to the British, there was no need to worry about a future generation of workers, British colonialism would ensure that there would be an endless supply.

The other effect of Family Wage was that by preserving the family, women were forced into a role as the 'servicers' of labour power – i.e. looking after male workers so that they would be in a fit condition to perform well for capitalism. In the case of the colonies wages were always extremely low, women in many parts of the world were expected to keep themselves and their families going by working on the land while men did wages work – the issue of servicing labour power did not arise in the same way because again all labour was seen as expendable and easily replaceable. This now has affected the British state's attitude to the black family. The 'servicing' of black labour power, the welfare costs for black workers, are being neither acknowledged nor met. The Bangladeshi family which bore the costs of producing the Bangladeshi worker and giving him continued emotional support is kept out of Britain. What it means is that Britain is refusing to meet the costs of servicing the workers whose labour it has used and is still using. What is most convenient for the state is when black workers, old and ill with occupational disease, have to retire to their country of origin driven out of Britain by the racism of everyday life. Then the final welfare costs of these workers again fall upon the ex-colonies they came from, absolving Britain of any duties or responsibilities.

Finally the Family Wage for British workers is a milestone in another process, the changing position and role of women within the British family. In a hundred years the family itself had changed from a peasant extended family to a nuclear crafts family (where women to start with played as important a part in the production process as men) to the establishment of a nuclear family unit with a male wage earner. The woman was then separated from the production process and given her role within capitalism of the day – as producer of future labour power and the servant and servicer of the male worker. These changes have been analysed by British feminists who have shown how they were crucial in developing and consolidating the ideology of the British family and establishing the woman's role. In the Indian sub-continent women, particularly in the urban areas, faced the first two steps – the change from peasant extended family to crafts workers – through the natural development of society but then when the society was poised on the brink of independent capitalist development, colonialism pushed it backwards into feudalism made all the harsher because it was the reversal of a natural process. It affected the woman's role profoundly, colonialism then is the key, the root cause not only of the poverty of Bangladesh but of the type of oppression faced by women in Bangladeshi society. Capitalism when it developed in Bangladesh, aside from colonial capitalism, was not for the benefit of the country itself but still in a mode functioning for neocolonial purposes. It meant uneven development where the men migrated to the towns in search of employment and women were left behind in the villages. Life was full of separation and sorrow. But at least these partings were not on the scale the British Immigration policy has enforced.

Colonialism as we have seen transformed India. A country full of vigour and affluence became a land of abject poverty and famine – a society poised on the brink of industrialisation was pushed back into relying on the overburdened agricultural system. The British also imposed their own legal and administrative system for extracting revenue and this changed India even further. Previously the Indian kings had taken a fixed proportion of produce as tax or tribute, now the British demanded a fixed sum of money depending not on produce but on the amount of land a peasant held – this was called rent and those who could not pay could be evicted. Essentially this meant that the peasants became tenants on their own land but what it also meant was that the person given the task of extracting the rent – the Zamindar – became enormously rich. He acted in addition as money lender, backed up in this by the British police and legal system. In this way extreme poverty and inequality became the underlying characteristics of the society. And it was poverty and powerlessness which forced people to accept a set-up where the family was often separated in their endless search for work and wages.

The Effects of Partition

With the great traditional cities of Dacca and Murshidabad declining, the British began to establish their own centres. In Bengal the major industrial centre was of course Calcutta which began to serve as the economic focus for the whole of Bengal.

The British partition of India – into India and Pakistan – led to the separation of West and East Bengal. It was a major economic blow for the East since it meant that it was suddenly cut off from its industrial heart. United Bengal might have developed into a major political force, partition reduced the possibility of this ever happening.

Separations

As for the Bengali family, well before partition, in fact soon after the establishment of Calcutta as an industrial centre, separations had become a part of everyday life. The men from villages and small towns – sons, newly married husbands, fathers – would go into the towns for weeks, months, sometimes as long as a year or two. It is a situation familiar in every third world country. Dawood Haider,[7] a poet from Bangladesh describes it in a poem written in the seventies.

> I LEFT YOU BEHIND
> I left you, my love,
>   I left you behind.
> Along with a worn out mat,
>   an oil aged pillow,
> two cracked pans, a basket,
>   and a rusty shovel
> I left you behind in a rotting hovel
> at the swampy edge
>   of the village.
>
> I remember what I meant
>   to say to you.
> I wanted to leave
>   you a few coins
> I wanted to tell
>   the Munshi House people
> to give you a job.
>   I wanted to leave you
> my scarf which you could wear
>   could wear besides
> your only tattered sari.
>   But I did not say
> or do any of these things,
>   I just left you behind.

However, behind the pain of these separations was hope of a better life together (although admittedly these hopes were not always fulfilled). There was also the assumption that such partings were for limited periods. This was also how Sylheti workers viewed their visits to Britain in the sixties. A family would send one son to earn some money for a few years, then he would return and be replaced by a brother or cousin. But the Immigration Acts with their strict control of entry of workers put an end to the process. That was why the

---

7. Dawood Haider, Take Me Home Rickshaw, Salamander.

wives and children of Bangladeshi workers finding themselves faced with permanent separation decided to come to this country to join their husbands and fathers. Every family now torn apart by the immigration laws have in common a tragic irony – the men came into Britain for the sake of their families, worked in the harshest conditions so they would have a better chance of survival – only to be parted from them for ever.

"Bangladesh Divided Families Campaign" demonstrating in London, where the Police refused permission to march to the Home Office

THE COTTON INDUSTRY IN BRITAIN

From Britain's point of view this new influx of workers was like a blood transfusion. Not only was this country short of workers in the boom which followed the second world war, but racism ensured that the new black workers were given the worst paid and most unpleasant jobs which white workers did not want to do. Many of these jobs were in the very textile industry which owed its development directly to the colonial loot and destruction of Bengal.

Oldham, where many Bangladeshi workers went to work in the sixties, is a typical textile town. In 1714 it was a large village with a population of 4,000. By 1801 the population was 12,024 and by 1901, 147,483. In 1794 Oldham had 12 mills whereas in 1884 there were 265. The conditions described by Engels (quoted earlier) had improved but hours were still very long, work unsafe and child labour was common. In terms of world trade the British textile industry reached a peak in 1912 (controlling nearly $2/3$). But after 1912 it began to decline. It picked up slightly after the 1914-1918 war but then slumped again in the face of competition from Japan and the failure to implement any modernisation. By the 1920s it had got left behind in terms of production and markets.

Ring spindles, which are essential for the production of cheap cotton goods for mass markets, were simply not introduced in Britain. After the second world war there was a slight improvement in the situation but manufacturers still refused to modernise or reorganise the industry. When advised to do so by the government, they resisted, blaming the then Labour government for interfering in private 'free' enterprise. Not surprisingly the 1950s saw another slump and in the early sixties (after the Cotton Industry Reorganisation Act of 1959) the industry finally began to reorganise encouraged by government grants. Mills were closed and some, though by no means all, old machinery was scrapped, more significantly small companies merged with others or were taken over by companies like Courtaulds to form the 4 or 5 giant companies which dominate textiles now. Despite this there was no really effective attempt to modernise, the only significant change being that night shifts and continuous shifts were instituted. This required a small amount of new machinery. It made the industry economically feasible for the next few years but that was all. A minimum was being spent in fact to wring a few more working years from the old machinery. So while Courtaulds for example spent £403 million between 1962 and 1969 only £40 million of this was on new plant. Obviously this philosophy also called for workers at the lowest possible wages and this was where the textile industry drew upon black labour from the ex-colonies, some mills refusing to modernise till they were sure that they had got their Pakistani and Bangladeshi workers. (The reorganisation also meant that yarn packages and bobbins were larger, another reason apart from the nightshift for preferring male workers to the females, who had till then constituted the bulk of the workforce of the low paid textile industry.)

We have seen why Bangladeshis were willing to come to Britain and take up these rotten jobs – why they were not in a position to choose anything better.

The textile bosses found them particularly suitable: Firstly because they were new to the country, and because racism divided them from the rest of the workforce they were particularly powerless. In fact their being forced into night-shift work gave rise to myths which were to be used against them for years – for example that they did not have the same family ties as English workers! Secondly, the bosses could rest assured that given the attitudes of textile unions (which after all were just as racist as everyone else) it was unlikely that they could take on the bosses on the side of the black workers.

The textile unions in Lancashire were in any case characterised by now by a remarkable 'loyalty' to their employers and a tendency to collaborate with them. Chris Beasdale[8] in a recent study points out "the textile union's era of militancy ended over a hundred years ago. Even the strikes at the end of the last century and the beginning of this were just defensive and not part of political struggle on a wider level. It was caused partly by the fact that senior workers at the mills often took on the function of both worker's representative and junior management. Disputes were seen as something personal which could be sorted out by individuals with the help of shop representatives, over-lookers or union officials with management. Asking for support from workers in other units was simply laughed at.

8. Chris Beasdale, Oldham Trade Union Research Centre.

The other reason for the textile union's lack of militancy is described by Oldham TRC – Trade Union Research Centre – (Ian Stubbs) "there is a long history of shared pride in the industry between the workers and the management. They were all Oldhamers or Rochdalians etc. and what Oldham and Rochdale and Shaw and Royton were was what the textile industry made them.... When the management said rationalisation was necessary, the worker adapted to new machines and consequent shift work, and finally when the same managements told them that there was no future for their mills they accepted that too with tragic resignation". However one interprets the workers' acceptance of closure – i.e. was it passivity or lack of choice – the fact remains that there were few struggles against closure. And Ian Stubbs goes on to describe how the shape and organisation of the textile unions made them inadequate to deal with the forces ranged against them.

"Traditionally unions in the textile industry were local and served a particular section of workers. There was a Bolton Card and Ring Room Operatives Association, a Bolton Weavers Association and so on. Every textile town had five or six unions, each with a rule book, each with an executive committee, each with a general secretary, each with an office. The recent history of these unions has been a story of continual amalgamation, but always too little and always too late. Even today the Amalgamated Textile Workers Union is a federation of nine autonomous districts, which has meant for example that negotiations for amalgamation with the general workers' unions have gone on and on, and have caused splits and divisions among the different districts.

A clearer impression of those small local unions can be gained from looking at just one of them. This is what the Oldham Provincial Union of Textile and Allied Workers looks like in 1984.

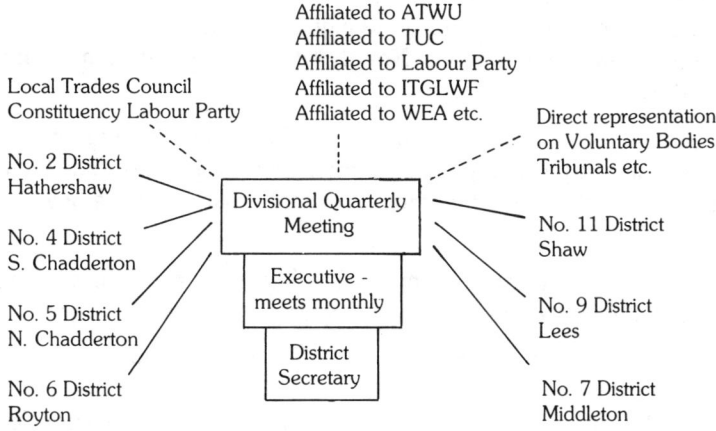

Each district has a Chairman – Secretary – Treasurer – Executive Representative – 5 Committee Members – 2 Auditors all elected annually.

35

There is no doubt that these local organisations did a remarkable job of representing the workers' rights to the nineteenth and early twentieth century mill owners and they take great pride in their strike-free record.

When Bangladeshi workers entered this system in the early sixties it was not really surprising that conditions of work were extremely unpleasant and unsafe.

Abdul Wahid who came in 1962 and worked 18 years in the cotton mills ended up with chronic bronchitis and an ulcer. (Even after this record of work he had to wait ten years before being allowed to bring his wife and son into this country.) Other workers were ill with Byssinosis. According the Oldham TRC "Byssinosis is one of the least known but longest standing industrial diseases. There are currently more than 3,000 confirmed sufferers and possibly twice the number who are unconfirmed. The disease is caused by the delicate passages of the lung being blocked by inhaled cotton dust and fibre. The symptoms are similar to bronchitis. Each week one former cotton worker dies and three more show symptoms of the disease. In the last 2 years government and companies have paid out more than £2 million in compensation or pensions."

But neither Abdul Wahid nor any other Bangladeshi worker we spoke to received any compensation.

Abdul Wahid told us that in his mill there were medical exminations on alternate years – this was despite the fact that annual checks of workers in the cotton industry were recommended way back in the 1930s.

"When I started working" says Abdul Wahid "it was night shift work – 10 pm to 6 am. Then for a few years it was multishift work, 7.30 am to 7.30 pm for 2 weeks and 7 pm to 7 am for 2 weeks. It was terribly disorientating. The days would be spent recovering from the nights, then just when you got used to it you would have to work days. Now of course there are no more multishifts. The industry has run down."

This account simply of a Bangladeshi worker's hours of work indicates how the textile industry has used black workers mercilessly – working them literally to sickness. At the same time the state is not willing to concede to them even the basic human right of family life.

The British textile industry meanwhile is still trying to make do with a minimum of modernisation expense and a maximum of exploitation.

"Now in some ways conditions are slightly better than they used to be, but in other ways they are worse. While in the old days there are two workers per machine looking after 2 sides or 440 bobbins, now one person looks after between 8 and 12 machines depending on the mill. Some mills, but only a few, have new Japanese machines, the rest still use the same old equipment."

IMMIGRATION AND NEO-COLONIALISM
Ibrahim Ali's case

Ibrahim Ali is from Hamidpur, a remote village in Bangladesh. He is in his fifties and for nearly half of his life has worked in the mills and factories of Manchester. Since 1972 he has been trying to bring his family into this country. In the years in between one son has died and two have passed the age when they qualify for entry into Britain. His wife and youngest son were given entry in 1977 but they had to return to look after the rest of the family.

Ibrahim Ali's case is unusual only in the details of its documentation which reveal in their own words, not only the racism of the British High Commission Officials, but their blatant colonial attitudes.

Ibrahim Ali's wife Marfush Bibi and their four sons applied for entry to Britain in early 1972. In the next two years they faced a shuttlecock of interviews (of the family in Dacca and Ibrahim Ali in Manchester), an intrusive sifting of the personal details of their lives and 'doubt' expressed by the ECOs as to the 'genuineness of their relationships'. There are discrepancies apparently as to the exact ages of the children – were they born after Ibrahim's first visit home or second? During the visit or after? And what about Ibrahim's daughters, who have not and never had applied to come to Britain? The High Commission officials wished to find out how old they were and when they got married. Were these questions relevant? The entry certificate officers thought they were. And since in Bangladesh there are no birth certificates and in rural areas dates are not considered crucial, it was easy for the ECOs to accuse this family, like so many others, of lying.

Finally in September 1973 after seven interviews the ECO's admitted that the family were all related as they said. But instead of issuing Entry Certificates they sent all the papers to the Home Office to be looked at again. There the file 'went astray' for nearly a year and when it was found and the entry certificates were about to be issued the ECO intervened again – two denunciatory letters had been received about Ibrahim's application. These letters, which meant that the case was reopened, were never seen. But this time the High Commission officials decided to undertake an epic journey to darkest Bangladesh – they would visit Hamidpur and discover the truth. ECO, M.J. Shingler chronicled this journey in great detail.

They set off in January 1977 but despite 'strenuous efforts' could not get through. In mid-February, two ECO's decided to try again. They arranged to take two interpreters, a Landrover, with driver, enough provisions for a week and camping equipment. In Sylhet town they met some doctors who were going to a health centre on the way to Hamidpur, and they decided to accompany them because 'local farmers in the area could be hostile to people driving over newly ploughed paddy fields'. Even so, the intrepid ECO's faced problems: 'It was very time consuming forging a new track over the paddy because the paddy field walls were too high in places for a Landrover, so we had to zig zag round to find the best way'; also some children 'threw half and quarter bricks at the Landrover'. In a village near Hamidpur an amazing thing happened: some villagers (identified only as A, B and C etc.) approached them and told them, without any prior conversation, that Ibrahim Ali was a liar and was not related to the people who had applied to come to Britain. At Hamidpur, this was angrily denied. But the ECO's spent no more than twenty minutes there and they were reluctant to question people 'because with the crowds involved in Hamidpur village it was essential that I tried to keep them at bay while Miss Byrde tried to keep ahead of the mass'.

The ECO's returned to Dacca and in March called the family back for interview. They told them that the two older sons Bashir and Ashique were not their sons and Ashique was not a Muslim at all, but came from a Hindu family who had promised to give Ibrahim land in return for taking their son to Britain. Proof of this, they said, was the fact that Ashique had not been circumcised. It was pointless Marfush Bibi pointing out that Ashique had not been circumcised because he had been suffering from acute eczema when the local circumcisor had come round to do the boys of the family. She was told that if she did not confess that Ashique and Bashir were not her sons then the third, Ala, would be refused entry. She answered that she did not care what Shingler said, as far as she was concerned they were all her sons.

Bashir, Ashique and Ala were then refused Entry Certificates. In the next few months Bashir died. His death certificate gives Ibrahim Ali as father. Ashique and Ala's appeal came up before the Adjudicator in Manchester in December 1979. Sushma, who represented the boys, produced four witnesses from Hamidpur who testified in court that the boys were Ibrahim's sons in contrast to the nameless villagers (A, B and C). Receipts were shown for the money Ibrahim had sent home in the names of his sons as far back as 1965, and it was pointed out that he had no motivation for bringing a Hindu boy to Britain because being a Muslim he could never use land in a Hindu village.

The Adjudicator did not answer these points. With a determination which matched the style and content of Shingler's report he dismissed the appeal. As for his own understanding of the intricacies of the case, he throughout referred to the youngest son as though he were a girl.

HOW THE HOME OFFICE POLICES BANGLADESH

Home Office village visits of the type described above represent a state agency spying on people in another country with the collusion of their government. Unlike other agencies which spy internationally like the KGB and CIA, the Home Office is quite open and self-righteous about its presence in a remote village in Bangladesh. Implicit in this is the assumption that the colonial past qualifies them to pass judgement both on individuals, who are seen as liars, and on a country which is seen as dishonest.

In fact the Home Office's behaviour most closely resembles that of a colonial police force which, for example, would follow workers on the tea plantations of Ceylon back to their homes in rural southern India in order to arrest them on charges brought against them by unscrupulous white plantation owners. And yet this does not prevent them from haggling or bargaining in the most petty and dishonest way as they did in Ibrahim Ali's case – we'll allow in two sons if you give up your claim to the third.

As an exercise in neo-colonial administration, village visits are worth looking at in more detail because they provide an insight into the British authorities' attitude to Bangladeshis.

The idea (of village visits) was originally a 'liberal' one thought up in fact, by a Home Secretary known for his compassion – Alex Lyon. They were seen as 'additional means of verifying the true facts in cases which it was felt were difficult if not impossible to resolve satisfactorily in Dacca'. But like so many other liberal initiatives which have ended up not only part of a racist set-up but serving to heighten racism, village visits have now become an integral part of the procedure whose aim is humiliation and exclusion. (Of course there is another kind of village visit too, the kind on which this book is based, but here we shall look at the Home Office variety.) The current Home Office approach to village visits is outlined in a paper by the Acting Second Secretary L. C. Taylor. The paper has been produced because although in the past "village visits were exclusively our province. However, increasingly, various bodies and organisations are now conducting similar enquiries on behalf of applicants and appellants. So far we have observed major flaws in many of these enquiries.... we have decided to set out in detail our methods of enquiry which have been established over the last eight years." In other words, disconcerted by the fact that independent village visits had actually helped people with a right to enter Britain to do so, the Home Office has decided to lay down rules as to how such visits should be conducted.

We reproduce a major part of their paper below:

The major advantage of conducting enquiries in the village is that we are able to speak to, and take evidence from the applicants' peers. Most Sylheti villages, particularly the smaller ones with fewer residents who have links with the United Kingdom, tend to be closely knit communities with each family knowing much about the affairs of others. We can speak to neighbours, school contemporaries and other villagers, in addition to local officials, such as the post master, school headmaster etc., who could be expected to know many of the villagers through their everyday contacts.

There are however difficulties in this type of investigation. The relative wealth and influence of families with relatives in the United Kingdom are such that, in some instances, villagers are reluctant to impart information for fear of recrimination. It is therefore essential to preserve the anonymity of villagers who have provided evidence, when referring to them in a public document, such as an appeal statement. Cases have also been encountered where villagers have been made aware of an attempted deception and proceed to name children whom a sponsor has previously admitted to be false. A further difficulty are cases where villagers deliberately offer misleading information. This could be the result of jealousies or grievances harboured against a wealthier, more influential neighbour. A major source of disputes in Sylheti villages concerns the ownership of land, which in the largely agrarian economy forms the basis of most villagers' livelihood. It is therefore particularly important to ensure at the outset of an interview, that no enmity exists between the villager and the family being investigated.

The season during which village visits can be successfully undertaken is brief, running from November to March, the cool dry season in Bangladesh. Visits

Protests in London

outside this period have been attempted in the past with only a limited degree of success. The climatic conditions throughout the monsoon season present a major obstacle and restrict visits to the few villages which remain accessible by metalled roads. With such a limited season at our disposal, we would normally expect to carry out no more than four trips during the season. These trips are costly, not only financially but also in terms of the number of man hours devoted to a single application. The actual number of cases listed for village visits must necessarily be restricted. Approximately 140 cases are listed each year, amounting to less than 2% of the total number of applications received during the same period. The decision to list a case may only be taken after reference to a Second Secretary, and the list is regularly reviewed. Inevitably, certain visits will prove to be impossible, usually for reason of poor accessibility. Occasionally, the results from a village visit prove inconclusive. In all such cases, a decision will be taken by applying the test of the balance of probabilities.

The village visit is undertaken by a team, usually consisting of 4 Entry Clearance Officers and two interpreters. (We ensure that native-born Sylheti interpreters are employed on all village visits.) The exercise is co-ordinated by a team leader, a senior ECO who will have had previous village visit experience. The team leader will have spent time in Dhaka preparing a work programme for the week. This will involve assembling the cases into the particular areas of the Sylhet district which the team plans to visit and establishing the approximate location of the villages concerned with the aid of ordinance survey maps and more recently acquired 'Thana' maps (Sylhet district is divided into some 30 separate 'Thanas'). Unfortunately, experience has shown that our maps are not always particularly accurate. However our interpreters and drivers have extensive knowledge of the district and only in cases involving the more far flung villages are we obliged to seek road-side guidance from the local inhabitants. The team leader is also responsible for organising transport, food and accommodation.

Entry Clearance Officers are under instructions, when submitting a case for a village visit, to prepare a facts sheet detailing the background of the application and the purpose of the proposed visit. The reasons for this are two-fold:
Firstly, it will enable the Second Secretary to assess the viability of the visit and secondly, it will give the team, working in the field, an outline of the case without the necessity of sorting through often long and involved files. Photographs of the applicants are also included whenever possible to assist villagers in making positive identification. Details of the applicants' immediate and extended family are provided in the form of a family tree. It is not unusual for

Village life

several inhabitants of the same village to bear similar or identical names. A family tree can help prevent mistaken identification at an early stage and enable the team to confirm family details provided by the applicants.

The success or failure of a village visit is to a large extent dependent on the element of surprise. It is therefore imperative that neither the applicants nor sponsor receive any forewarning of a planned visit, for to do so would entirely negate the findings of this form of investigation. This also extends to the local authorities and police, none of whom are advised of our village visit programmes. If the applicants were to suspect or have fore-knowlege of an impending visit, it would be an easy matter for them to influence or persuade their fellow villagers to provide a corroborative account of their family details. It is a fact that families with 'Londoni' connections (relatives in the United Kingdom) can and do wield considerable influence in the average Sylheti village. It is by no means impossible for a wealthy sponsor to ensure that collusion takes place throughout an entire village. It is primarily for these reasons that we are unable to accede to any requests from applicants to carry out local enquiries. To carry out a pre-announced visit would accomplish little more than to transfer the interview from an office situation to the village.

The area to be visited will be selected on the eve of the visit by the team leader and the members of the team will be given an opportunity to examine the cases set down for that area. A team can rarely accomplish more than four visits in a day, although as many as eight cases may be prepared in advance. Certain villages may prove to be inaccessible and it is therefore essential to have a number of 'standby' cases.

The arrival of a group of Europeans at a Sylhet village is by no means an everyday event. It will take very little time to attract the attention of a sizeable crowd of curious inhabitants unless this part of our operation is carried out swiftly and efficiently. The team therefore immediately separates into two parties, each with its own interpreter. The first party, whom I will refer to as the 'compound party', then sets off rapidly in the direction of the village, enlisting en route the assistance of a villager to direct them to the sponsor's compound. Whilst every effort is made, at this stage, to ensure that the subject of our enquiry is not divulged to any interested parties, speed is nevertheless of the essence in order to arrive at the compound ahead of anyone wishing to forewarn the family concerned (commonly known as 'the runner').

At the subject's compound the team will take note of all those present on the compound and establish the reasons for absences of any of the applicants. A frequent explanation offered for the absence of an applicant or non-applicant is that they are away "visiting relatives" or "out working in the fields". Whilst such explanations may well be true, experience has taught us to regard these answers with a degree of circumspection. The sudden appearance of an applicant "from the fields" does not necessarily confirm the relationship. It is an easy matter for someone to fetch the applicant from his real father's house on a neighbouring compound.

It is normal practice to make a rough diagram of the compound and, with the assistance of an applicant or a close relative of the family, to detail the occupants of each room. Permission would then be obtained to view the rooms and examine them for evidence of occupancy e.g. school books bearing the occupant's name, clothing, photographs etc.

Whilst the compound team is thus engaged, the second party, whom I shall refer to as the 'walkabout team', will have allowed the compound team to gain a head start before setting off to make enquiries in and around the village, avoiding the compound belonging to the subjects of the enquiry. Villagers are chosen at random during the walkabout and every effort is made to interview them as privately as possible. In smaller, scattered communities conducting such interviews may pose few problems. However in the more densely populated communities it becomes difficult to prevent a crowd of curious onlookers gathering during an interview. In this situation, the presence of the second ECO is invaluable. Whilst one ECO is engaged in conducting an interview at a distance, the other can hold the attention of any followers by taking photographs, conversing with an English speaking member of the group and generally 'entertaining' the crowd.

The walkabout team would avoid interviewing any villager who pressed his attentions on them, as such a person may well be related to, or acting on the instructions of the sponsor. Alternatively, he may be in dispute with subjects of the enquiry and seek to provide misleading information. They would also avoid interviewing groups of villagers and unaccompanied children under 14 years of age. In the case of the former pressure may be brought to bear on the individual being questioned by other members of the group and coaching or encouragement may be offered. In the latter case, it is a matter of policy arising from our experience that evidence obtained from young children can prove unreliable.

At the commencement of an interview the ECO would first obtain details of the interviewee's name, age, occupation and length of residence in the village. The latter point is particularly important since only long term inhabitants of the village can be expected to have detailed knowledge of the fellow villagers' domestic affairs. Photographs of the applicants would then be produced for identification. If the villager is able to identify the photographs, the ECO would then establish whether any enmity existed between the interviewee and those depicted in the photographs. The ECO would then proceed to question the villager on the family details of those concerned. A similar procedure would be followed in the event that the villager was unable to identify the photographs. Although the catalyst in this case would be the sponsor's name or the names of any of his brothers.

Generally we find that villagers are less inhibited in their own surroundings and will freely discuss the affairs of others. Their knowledge, particularly concerning older male members of a family, can be quite extensive. However it is unusual for older villagers to be familiar with the details of young children (under 10 years old) or female members of a family (including the principal applicant). We consider that unequivocal statements obtained from villagers in this fashion can provide strong evidence in support of or against a claimed relationship.

There are no set instructions as to the number of villagers who should be interviewed. That is left to the team's discretion. Clearly, however, it would be unreasonable to base conclusions on the interviews of only one or two villagers. However a true picture of the family can sometimes be gained at an early stage by the the compound party, and it is not unknown for admissions to be made concerning the applicants by those present on the compound. In these circumstances the position can be communicated to the walkabout team via short wave radios and thus help prevent an excessively long and unnecessary investigation. Similarly the walkabout team can 'radio-in' the results of their investigation whilst that prt of the enquiry is still in progress.

Once a relationship has been satisfactorily established, the walkabout team would then proceed to the applicants' house where they would join the compound team. Here, they would confront the applicants, and sponsor if he is present, with their findings, thus providing an opportunity for the family concerned to offer explanations where our enquiries have revealed the claimed relationships to be false. Additional enquiries at schools or the local Mosque may be conducted at this stage by the whole team.

Throughout the course of the village visit full details of the enquiry will be taken down in note form, or with the aid of dictaphones. On return to 'base' in the evening the team will write-up the results of their investigations for that day and submit a recommendation for decision. The team would also discuss and evaluate their findings, particularly in the more complex visits, where the results may not have been entirely conclusive. Immediate write-up is clearly essential whilst the details of the enquiries remain fresh in the minds of the team.

By and large our reception at the villages is open and friendly and we are anxious that it should remain this way. However, with an ever increasing number of visits being undertaken by other bodies, we are concerned that the villagers will become wary of our presence and that the value of these visits will gradually be undermined. We are already discovering that frquent visits to the same village result in less than conclusive evidence.

The list of rules must be followed when conducting village visits:

i) The applicants and sponsor should receive no forewarning of an intended visit.

ii) The village visit team should consist of a minimum of four investigators, assisted by two native-born Sylheti interpreters.

iii) A case history of the application, together with full family details and, whenever possible, photographs of the applicants should be available.

iv) The subjects of the enquiry should not be announced immediately on arrival at the village.

v) The team should divide into two parties and one party should proceed as quickly as possible to the sponsor's house in order to arrive there ahead of any 'runner'.

vi) The walkabout team should cover a wide area of the village, avoiding the sponsor's compound.

vii) The team should endeavour to interview local inhabitants individually and privately. A second investigator is essential in these circumstances to ensure privacy for the interviewer.

viii) The team should always establish the interviewee's length of residence in the village and whether he is in dispute with the subjects of the enquiry.

ix) The walkabout team should avoid interviewing relatives of the applicants, unaccompanied children under the age of 14 and anyone who insisted upon being questioned.
x) Notes or recordings should be taken at all times and they should be transcribed at the earliest opportunity.
xi) The walkabout and compound teams should remain in communication at all times.
xii) Frequent visits to the same village should be avoided.

Village visits are undoubtedly very costly in terms of manpower and finances and, for the ECOs concerned, are hard work! However they remain an invaluable training exercise, as well as a means of resolving a number of our more complex applications.

L. C. TAYLOR
Acting Second Secretary

The significance of the Home Office guidance can be most clearly understood in the light of cases like that of Ibrahim Ali: Neocolonialism essentially gives a country economic and political power over another. This power is exercised indirectly. But British officials' casual contempt of Bangladeshi authorities and police shows that this power is being quite openly exercised. It surfaces again and again. For example in the case of Irshad Ali the ECO's curt comment "I could place no reliance on these or other documentary evidence"; or in the case of Abdul Wahid where the ECO "placed no weight on documents produced, namely a copy of the land deed purporting to transfer land from the sponsor's father to the sponsor's first wife as substitute dower; a school certificate in respect of Ashraf and a certificate from the Chairman of the Union Council to the effect that the appellants were the sons of the sponsor and known to him. He (the ECO) considered that such documents could be easily bought by a wealthy sponsor. He accordingly refused the application."

There is in addition the cool assumption that Britain's colonial past gives immigration officers the right to pry into people's private lives without even consulting the Bangladeshi authorities. For example: "It is normal practise to make a rough diagram of the compound with the assistance of an applicant or a close relative of the family to detail the occupants of each room. Permission would then be obtained to view the rooms and examine them for evidence of occupancy e.g. schoolbooks bearing the occupant's name, clothing, photographs etc." Just how such 'permission was obtained' was described to us by Chowdhary who has since been trying to bring his son into Britain "My father had just died and we were in the middle of the period of mourning, my wife and I were staying in our house in the village. My eldest who was 12, had an exam and had to stay on in town (in our house in Dacca). He was alone there when the British officials turned up without any notice. They insisted on going into all the rooms and asking all sorts of questions. They began to sort through all our old photographs and examine all the school reports and all private papers they could lay their hands on. Then they left for the bazaar where also they questioned people about us. The whole process was ridiculous but it was also humiliating."

RACIST HUMILIATION THROUGH 'MEDICAL' TESTS

Despite the British officials' unconcealed contempt of the Bangladeshi authorities, these authorities show them the utmost co-operation. Civil servants and ex-civil servants make every effort to satisfy their every demand in a manner which is as condescending in the treatment of the people as it is servile to the British. Most well-known among these civil servants is the legendary Dr. Latif, the High Commission Medical Advisor, whose 'age estimates' play such a crucial role in the exclusion of Bangladeshi women and children. Latif is described by M. J. Towsby (ECO in Ajibun Nessa and Jitu Miah's case) as "an eminent local doctor, formerly Senior House Physician at Dacca Medical College. He uses K. N. Baksh's Synopsis of Medical Jurisprudence which is the main reference text used by medical colleges in this country. Dr. Baksh was born in Bengal and his text, as revised by Bangladeshi doctors, deals with people of the sub-continent with particular reference to those born in Bengal. The author acknowledges references to Lyon's Medical Jurisprudence and for India Taylor's Principle and Practise of Medical Jurisprudence and Glaister's Medical Jurisprudence and Toxicology."

In other words Dr. Latif uses books which not only take into account the peculiarities of natives but are sound medically since they are at least partly based on the work of British doctors like Taylor and Glaister. In Bangladesh Towsby goes on to tell us "because of the lack of accurate and reliable documentation, age estimation has of necessity become an exact science. Local doctors take into account all of the facts which may affect age estimation and their estimates are accepted by the Bangladeshi government as a reasonable basis on which official documents such as passports and birth certificates may be issued where there is no other evidence of age." This use of such 'medical' evidence to judge age by the Bangladeshi government is of course different from the use to which ECOs and immigration officers are putting it. Because if the age on a passport or birth certificate is inaccurate it does not necessarily affect the whole of a person's life whereas in immigration cases even slight discrepancies in age can lead the authorities to the conclusion that the person and his or her sponsor are liars – which in turn can lead to exclusion. In addition of course there is an age bar, children over the age of 18 are simply denied entry.

"The doctor", Nosira Banu, Hamdu Miah's wife explained "is part of the High Commission. He has a room there and the officials send you to him. You pay him usually about Rs 410 for X-ray and medical report for one person (although it can be more). That is all, one can't ask questions, one can't ask

49

what the fee is for? or are there any lady doctors? Anyhow there are no lady doctors at all connected with the whole business."

The doctor in the High Commission is the High Commission Medical Advisor (a post created it appears with this special work in mind). In addition of course there is the local Civil Surgeon and radiologists and they too are usually willing to oblige the High Commission. The 'medical' examination has two main aspects – X-rays and sexual examinations – both apparently used to assess age. People's basic human rights are being determined on the basis of arbitrary physical characteristics. And despite the much publicised stopping of 'virginity tests' these sexual examinations to 'test age' go on unchecked.

Despite all the trivial information about Bangladeshi customs collected by British ECOs, despite their avid interest in the Bangladeshi family, these examinations are still performed by male doctors – revealing their true purpose – the humiliation and harassment of Bangladeshi women. In a recent case of an adolescent girl trying to join her father, the ECO Towsby went out of his way to show his implicitly racist anthropological familiarity with Sylheti customs and use this half baked knowledge to argue against the appellant. "The villages of Sylhet have a subsistence level economy. Men do not marry until they have established a station in life.... conversely daughters are a liability.... they are married off as soon as they reach maturity... i.e. 16-17, so that men normally marry women considerably younger than themselves. In this case the sponsor's wife is just two years his junior. This is hardly likely in the male dominated society which exists here"; or later in the same case the remark "I had considered it unlikely bearing in mind the poverty of the Sylhet region that there were any real twins in the family". Towsby then set about 'proving' this assertion. For this he decided to seek the further advice of the High Commission Medical Advisor. A sexual examination was performed on the girl – is it possible that he did not know the implications of such an examination for a girl who had never before left her village in rural Sylhet?

With clinical coldness Towsby then recorded the main points of the 'medical report' on this fourteen year old girl.

"Pubic hairs appear at 12 and are present, axilla hairs appears at 12/13 and are present, menstruation in girls starts at 12/13 and has already started. External genitals are developed at 13 and had already developed".

At the British High Commission where all these forms of humiliation occur everyday it is hardly surprising that there is an overwhelming atmosphere of racism and contempt. According to one member of the team which visited Bangladesh from Manchester Law Centre "the officials at the High Commission were committed to the exclusion of as many people as possible. They displayed a particularly vicious form of racism where they both despised and suspected all applicants. This together with the tremendous amount of power they had, created a sort of paranoia – Bangladeshi people were thought of as 'illegal' by definition".

Bangladesh: the wife and child of the campaigner pictured on page 32; the local bank manager confirmed her identity

PARANOIA

Paranoia is of course crucial to British Immigration policy. It is whipped up among the white working class through cool and calculated propaganda to make them believe that excluding black people from Britain will benefit them. But paranoia is also now an integral part of the immigration system because officials with a normal sense of justice and humanity would find it hard to implement such a system. The fact that everything is handled, assessed and eventually judged by the same people allows this racist paranoia to grow unchecked. It permeates every part of the immigration system constantly feeding on itself, throwing up new reasons for suspicion and exclusion and new ways of categorising these rural women and children as immoral and dishonest and therefore not fit to enter Britain.

These attitudes emerge starkly in the reports written by ECOs. These worthy officials reveal that they see themselves as detectives moving with care to catch criminals of immense cunning or as missionaries out to save Britain from this immoral influx. In order to do this they not only humiliate and torture (as through the sexual examinations) but carry out characteristic interrogations – where every member of the family, even children as young as eleven, is questioned separately about subjects which are both irrelevant and unsubstantial.

The table from the ECO's report in Rushom Ali's case illustrates the process.

QUESTION	AYESHA BIBI	RUSHOM ALI	ALTAB ALI
Are any of the daughters married?	Yes, all are and all have children. I don't know their husband's or children's names.	I do not know if any of them are married.	Yes, all are married and have children but I don't know husbands' or children's names and ages.
To whom is Torik Ali (Ayesha Bibi's only brother married?	Aka Bibi	Don't know.	Don't know.

Have they any children?	None alive and none died.	None alive. I don't know if any died.	Same as Rushom
Did Asad ever go to school – details please?	Asad attended the Village Primary School. He left the V.P.S. 1 year ago. I do not know up to which class he read. He is not studying now.	He studies for his B.A. in a college in Sylhet Town. Sure? Yes.	He read up to Class 2 in the village primary school and left 8-10 years ago.
But he is allegedly 24 years old? And you say he left the V.P.S. only 1 year ago?		No reply.	
What is Rasad Ali's wife's name?	Nurful	Don't know.	Nurful
What is Rushom Ali's call name?	Siraj Miah	Don't know.	Don't know
What is your youngest daughter's/sister's name	Janu Bibi	Janu Bibi	Ranu Bibi
How old is she? Sure?	1 year Yes	5-6 years Well, maybe 4 years.	5-6 years Maybe 4 years.
Who was Mosrob Ali married to?	Don't know.	Don't know.	Don't know.
How old is Mosrob Ali's only son Ratik Ali?	60 years.	50-60 years.	50-60 years.
How old is Ratik Ali's eldest son, Elkas?	8-9 years.	15-16 years.	15-16 years.

53

QUESTION	AYESHA BIBI	RUSHOM ALI	ALTAB ALI
How old is Ratik Ali's 2nd son Sukur Ali?	6-7 years.	13-14 years.	13-14 years.
How old is Alesa Bibi daughter of Ratik Ali?	11 years.	18-19 years. Sure? Yes.	18-19 years. Sure? Yes.
To whom is Husena Bibi, daughter of Mosrob Ali married?	Touklis Miah	Don't know.	Touklis Miah
How many children has Husena Bibi?	1 son 3 daughters.	1 son 3 daughters.	1 son 3 daughters.
What are their names?	Son: Huson Miah Daughters: Peara Bibi Monwara Bibi Sitara Bibi	Same (10-11). Same.	Same. (Don't know age) Same.

In this process of interrogation with one meaningless trick question following another, truth and lies about these unsubstantial issues get completely mixed up. Sometimes appellants do lie if only because they feel that by doing so they will be able to extract themselves from the maze of questions which although they mean so little could so drastically affect their lives. There is a feeling of utter confusion deliberately created by the Immigration staff. For example (para 6 of ECO Salton's report on Sunara Begum/Irshad Ali's case).

"I asked the principal appellant why these documents had not been produced earlier but she said she did not know. I pointed out that the sponsor had said at a previous interview that these latter documents did not exist but she said she did not know. I suggested to her that these must therefore be bogus but again she said that she did not know. I then asked her a series of questions which I later put to Monir. Sunara said she had last seen her eldest son Ashik in the village. Monir agreed. Sunara said Ashik was wearing a white lungi and a multicoloured shirt where monir said he was wearing a green lungi and a white vest. Sunara said Ashik had accompanied them to the terminus where they had caught the bus for Biswanath, whereas Monir said Ashik had stayed home in the compound. Sunara said that her eldest daughter Zaheda slept in a room with Rupjan Bibi the sponsor's mother whereas Monir said that Zaheda slept with her sister Khaleda. Neither could remember what Zaheda was wearing when they left the compound but Sunara said that Khaleda was wearing a dark blue sari, whereas Monir said it was white.

People's illiteracy or unfamiliarity with essentially British legal procedures are used shamelessly to prove them liars. For example in Abdul Hashim and Amina Bibi's case among the 'unsatisfactory aspects of the case' which led to refusal and was so listed by the adjudicator was:

"The child Fulbahar was omitted from another form submitted in connection with the application, whereas all the other children were included. The explanation of the principal appellant, Amina Bibi, being illiterate was given, and that she would not have known that the person completing the form for her had omitted the name. But as the respondent's representative commented (i.e. the Home Office lawyer) in his submission, it is only to be expected that true parents would take all necessary steps to ensure that all their children were included. Dealing with this aspect of the matter the sponsor Abdul Hashim at first said 'I gave all the names on the form' and when it was pointed out that he was in the UK at the time he replied 'I don't know who completed it, my wife is illiterate'."

It is at the final stage of an appeal (the adjudication) that the true nature of the immigration process is fully revealed. Like in the inquisitions of the witchmania in the 17th century, where the accused would have to prove that they were not in league with the devil, and where the Inquisitor's pronouncement defined once and for all the accused person's 'morality' and their right to live. So in the adjudications or the immigration trials, the sponsor and appellants are accused persons and the adjudicator's determination is a judgement, not on the factual truth of the matter, but on the sponsor's and applicant's 'morality', which alone determines their legal position. What is at stake in this case of course is the tearing apart for ever of a mother and her children or a husband and wife.

Countless cases demonstrate how morality appears to be the same thing as credibility, or as performance as a witness. In Irshad Ali/Sunara Begum's case the Adjudicator actually commented that "establishing the truth was less important than the sponsor's performance as a witness". In Ashraf Ullah/Molukjan Bibi's case the Adjudicator summed up the ECO's criteria for rejection as follows: "only one discrepancy arose on the family tree, and apart from doubts as to an affidavit submitted in support, the decision appears to have been based on age estimates, a sparse family tree and marriage at an age earlier than normal" and rejected the appeal because "of the impression given by the sponsor's oral evidence" – he "laughed" and was "light-hearted" during the hearing. In the case of Chand Miah trying to bring his son Rushom Ali into Britain, the Adjudicator C.P.R. commented "from the point of view of the quality of the (oral) evidence this was one of the most unsatisfactory appeals I can recall. The sponsor hesitated long before answering and was clearly very nervous spending much time twisting his hands and fingers together.... The points at issue and the family circumstances were dealt with only in a sketchy manner. At one stage in his submission the appellant's representative said that he had not gone into the discrepancies noted by the Entry Clearance Officer because the sponsor had not been present at the interviews (i.e. interrogations). This approach frankly surprised me, and as the burden of proof is on the appellant, it is up to him or his representative to deal with at least the bulk of the discrepancies noted by the Entry Clearance Officer, and in the evidence to give me a substantial statement of the family relationships and domestic circumstances and background. In this way an Adjudicator is able to feel that whatever the discrepancies and other shortcomings, there is substantial evidence of a genuine family. The sponsor's wife was an elderly and very simple lady and I felt that she had little conception of what the proceedings were about".

Hamdu Miah's case is one where the issue of admitting his children to Britain became totally determined by the ECO's and Adjudicator's opinion of his general morality. His "lack of frankness" is noted and there are several references to his own right to be here both morally and legally (he jumped ship before 1962 and is therefore here entirely legally). For example we are told "within a few months of his arriving here, he obtained work, and although there have been periods of unemployment, he has been in work most of the time since. He is now 63 and is still at work".

Hamdu Miah had originally applied to bring his three sons Toymus Ali, Suba Miah and Tara Miah into Britain. Toymus was adopted as a baby and brought up as their own son to the extent of even being breast fed by Nosira Banu. His application however was rejected. Toymus then decided not to appeal against this decision and not to apply to come to Britain. When Hamdu Miah applied again to bring Suba and Tara, Toymus' original application was held against them. The Adjudicator's comment demonstrates how the entire process is being made dependent on the morality of the sponsor and applicant as assessed by the immigration system:

"Hamdu Miah has shown himself to be willing to attempt the illegal entry of a false dependent. He had not only perpetrated this deceit throughout the first application, but also before an Adjudicator at an appeals hearing. The applicants have shown themselves to be compliant accomplices in this deceit."

Finally there is the judgement in the case of Monar Ali, Arostal Bibi and their five children. The Adjudicator accepts that Arostal Bibi is the wife of Monar Ali and that four of the children are hers. But – "she applied under an assumed identity" and the conclusion is "I judge Monor Alito be of limited intelligence and do not discount the possibility of some kind of misunderstanding at this part of the interview". The appeal was rejected.

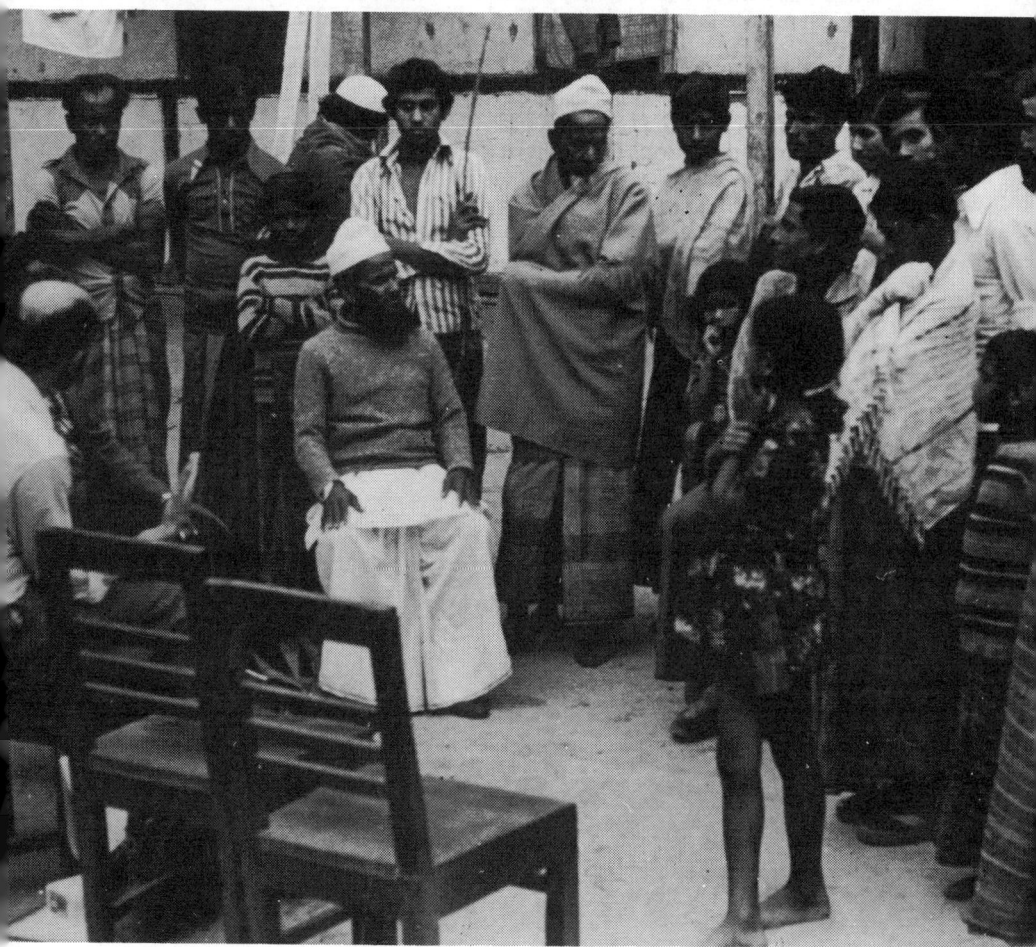

The schoolmaster is interviewed

The following publications are available from Manchester Law Centre. All prices include postage and packing.

1. **'WOMEN – HOW TO GET AN INJUNCTION'** – published in conjunction with the National Women's Aid Federation. This book deals with the legal remedies to domestic violence. — 45p
2. **'HOMELESS'** – this is a short guide to the Homeless Persons' Act. — 30p*
3. **'HOUSING REPAIRS – TENANTS' RIGHTS – LANDLORD'S RESPONSIBILITIES** – This book shows how landlords who refuse to do repairs can be taken to Court. This is not just private landlords but also includes Councils who fail to do repairs. — 70p*
4. **'THE LAW AND SEXUALITY'** – how to cope with the law if you are not 100% conventionally heterosexual. — £1.30p*
5. **'MATERNITY RIGHTS POSTERS'** – These are 5 posters which show in cartoons the rights of mothers and how they can protect their return to work. — £1.00
6. **'THE THIN END OF THE WHITE WEDGE'** – This book tries to analyse the effects of the new Nationality Laws and how they are creating a second class citizenship. — £1.00*
7. **'FROM ILL TREATMENT TO NO TREATMENT'** – A book inspired by the new health regulations which shows how health is becoming part of a package of internal controls. — £1.50*
8. **'EDUCATION AND DOLE'** – A guide to Benefits for students. — 75p*
9. **'OUR LIVES'** – Lesbian mothers talk to Lesbian mothers. — 80p*

*Those books numbered 2, 3, 6, 7, 8, 9 can be ordered by bookshops on trade terms through Scottish and Northern Book Distribution.

7. **Skull:**
   Sutures: Just started closing
   Bony Union of Sphenoid & Occipital:
   " " " " Styloid Process & Temporal:
   " " " " Pisiform bone:
   " " " " Ulna:

8. **Cervical Vertebrae:**
   Bony Union of Odontoid & Axis:
   " " " " Rami & Vertebrae dentata:

9. **Clavicle:** Fusion of Sternal end:

10. **Chest:** Fusion of Xiphoid Process & Sternum:
    Union of Manubrium & body:
    " " " Costal Cartilages:

I have examined F... B... on the basis of the foregoing and my estimate of this person's age is about/between

Results to: MACKAY
Entry Certificate Officer
BRITISH HIGH COMMISSION
DACCA

(Dr Abdul Latif)
Date: 28/5/77

Revised January 1977

-2-

RADIOLOGICAL FEATURES:

1. **Pelvis & Hip:**
   Bony Union of 1st sacral vertebrae and rest of sacrum: *Already occurred* — just completed
   " " Iliac crest: *Already occurred.*
   " " Ischeal Tuberosity: *Already occurred.*
   " " Head of femur: *Already occurred.*
   " " Rami of Pubis & Ischium:
   " " 3 portions of OS in ominatum:

2. **Knee:**
   Bony Union of Proximal end of Tibia, Febula:
   " " Distal end of Femur:

3. **Ankle:**
   Bony Union of Head of Humerus:
   "Two bony" points of Head of Humerus:

5. **Elbow:**
   Bony Union of medial epicondyl of Humerus:
   " " lateral " " :
   " " Head of Radius:

6. **Wrist:**
   Bony Union of Distal end of Radius: